JOHN THOMPSON'S
EASIEST PIANO COURSE

FIRST DISNEY FAVORITES

Arranged by Christopher Hussey

Disney Artwork TM and © 2019 Disney

ISBN 978-1-5400-6765-4

EXCLUSIVELY DISTRIBUTED BY

WILLIS MUSIC

HAL•LEONARD®

Visit Hal Leonard Online at
www.halleonard.com

Contact us:
Hal Leonard
7777 West Bluemound Road
Milwaukee, WI 53213
Email: info@halleonard.com

In Europe, contact:
Hal Leonard Europe Limited
42 Wigmore Street
Marylebone, London, W1U 2RY
Email: info@halleonardeurope.com

In Australia, contact:
Hal Leonard Australia Pty. Ltd.
4 Lentara Court
Cheltenham, Victoria, 3192 Australia
Email: info@halleonard.com.au

T0057862

I See the Light

from TANGLED

Music by Alan Menken
Lyrics by Glenn Slater

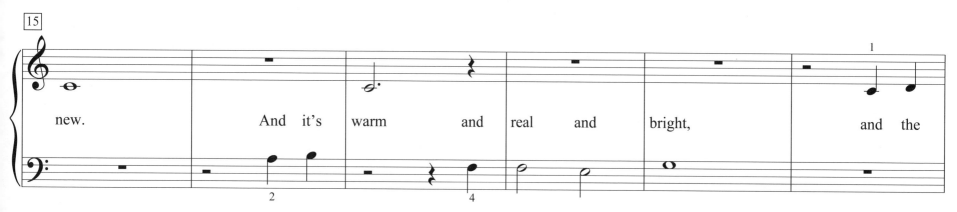

new. And it's warm and real and bright, and the

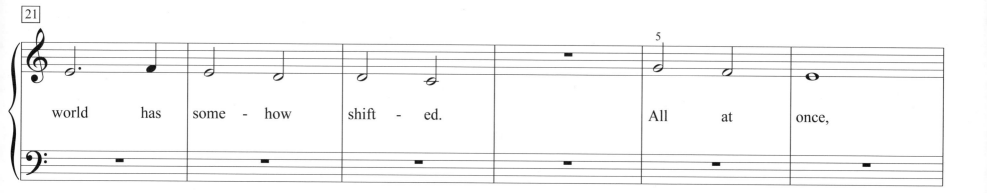

world has some - how shift - ed. All at once,

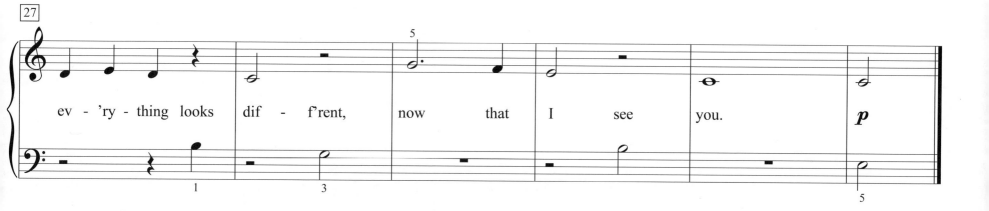

ev - 'ry - thing looks dif - f'rent, now that I see you. *p*

Let It Go
from FROZEN

Music and Lyrics by Kristen Anderson-Lopez
and Robert Lopez

Powerfully

Let it go, _____ let it go. _____ Can't hold it back

an - y - more. Let it go, _____ let it go.

Turn a - way _____ and slam _____ the door. _____

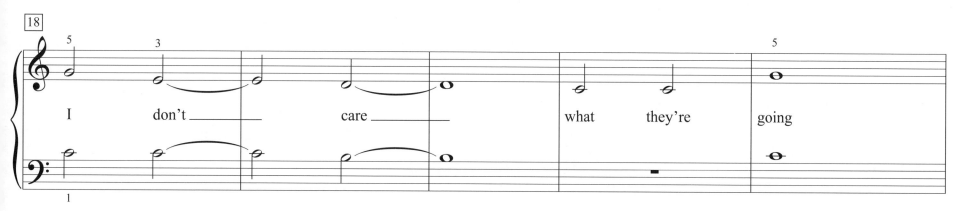

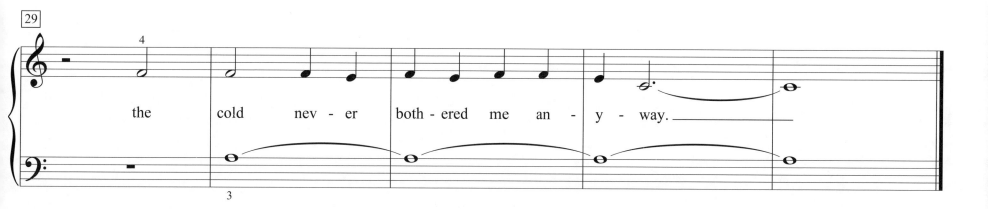

Colors of the Wind

from POCAHONTAS

Music by Alan Menken
Lyrics by Stephen Schwartz

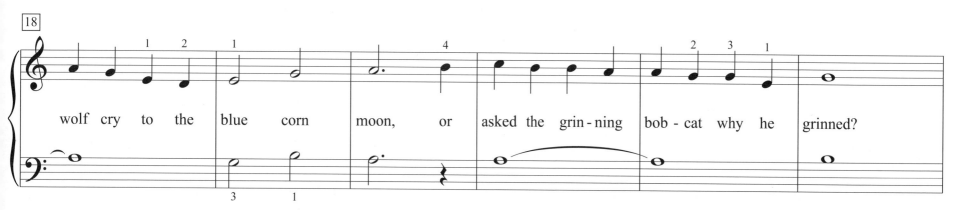

wolf cry to the blue corn moon, or asked the grin-ning bob-cat why he grinned?

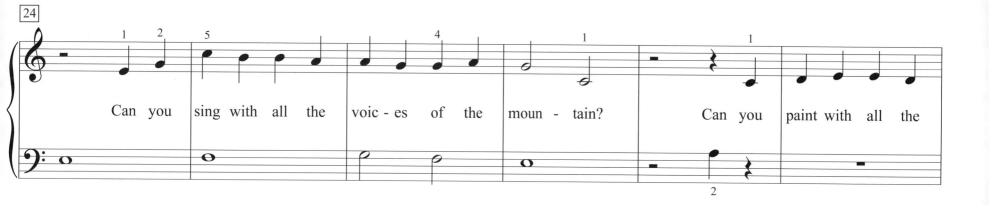

Can you sing with all the voic-es of the moun-tain? Can you paint with all the

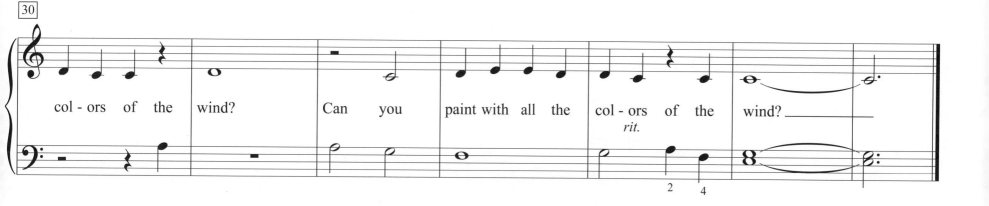

col-ors of the wind? Can you paint with all the col-ors of the wind? _____

rit.

Supercalifragilisticexpialidocious

from MARY POPPINS

Words and Music by Richard M. Sherman
and Robert B. Sherman

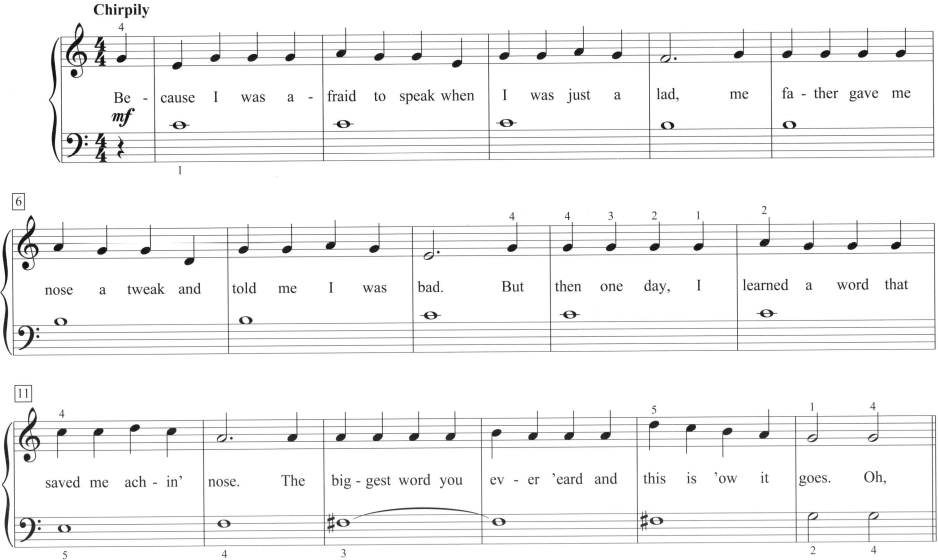

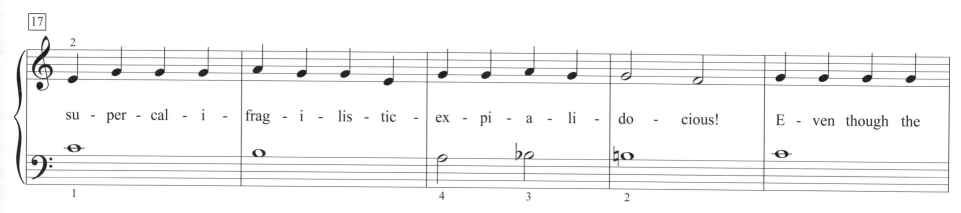

Remember Me
(Ernesto de la Cruz)
from COCO

Music and Lyrics by Kristen Anderson-Lopez
and Robert Lopez

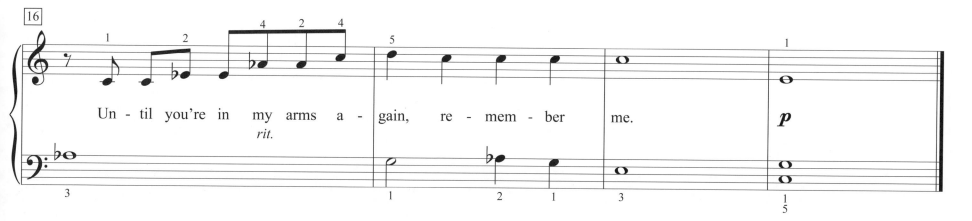

I Just Can't Wait to Be King

from THE LION KING

Music by Elton John
Lyrics by Tim Rice

13

Under the Sea
from THE LITTLE MERMAID

Music by Alan Menken
Lyrics by Howard Ashman

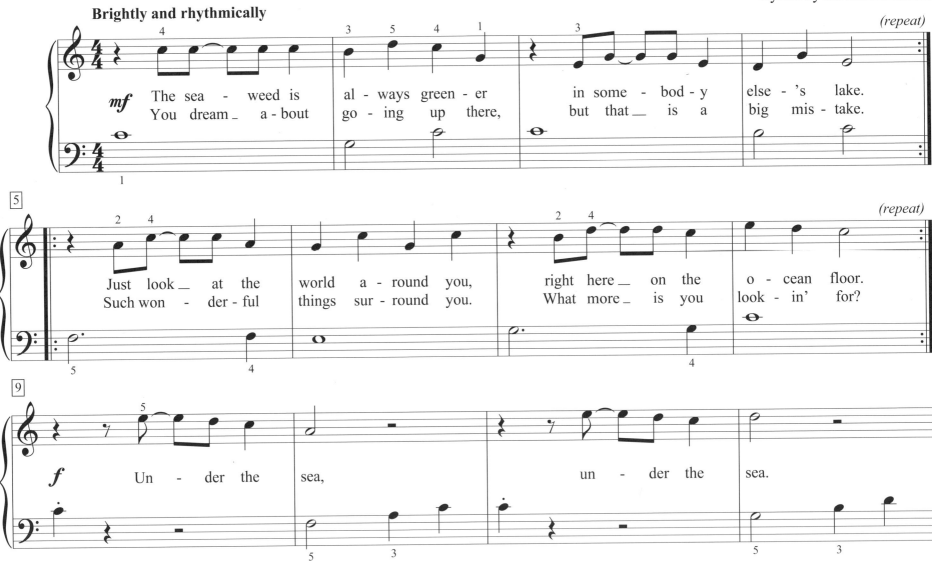

Brightly and rhythmically

mf

The sea - weed is al - ways green - er in some - bod - y else - 's lake.
You dream _ a - bout go - ing up there, but that _ is a big mis - take.

Just look _ at the world a - round you, right here _ on the o - cean floor.
Such won - der - ful things sur - round you. What more _ is you look - in' for?

f Un - der the sea, un - der the sea.

Dar - ling, it's bet - ter down — where it's wet - ter. Take — it from me.

Up — on the shore, they work — all day. Out — in the sun, they slave — a -

way while — we de - vot - in' full - time to float - in' un - der the sea.

He's a Pirate

from PIRATES OF THE CARIBBEAN: THE CURSE OF THE BLACK PEARL

Written by Hans Zimmer,
Klaus Badelt and Geoff Zanelli

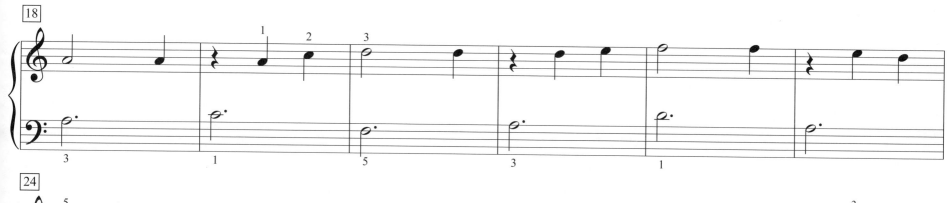

The Bare Necessities

from THE JUNGLE BOOK

Words and Music by
Terry Gilkyson

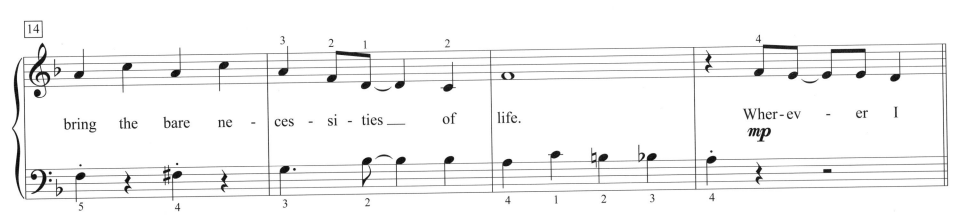

bring the bare ne - ces - si - ties ___ of life. Wher - ev - er I

mp

wan - der, wher - ev - er I roam, I could - n't be

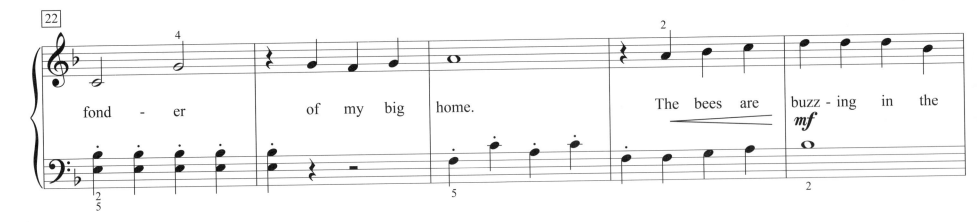

fond - er of my big home. The bees are buzz - ing in the

mf

tree to make some hon - ey just for me. When you look un - der the rocks and plants and

take a glance at the fan - cy ants, then may - be try a few. The bare ne -

ces - si - ties of life will come to you, they'll come to you.

You've Got a Friend in Me
from TOY STORY

Music and Lyrics by
Randy Newman

you've got a friend in me. Yes, you've got a friend in me. And as the years go

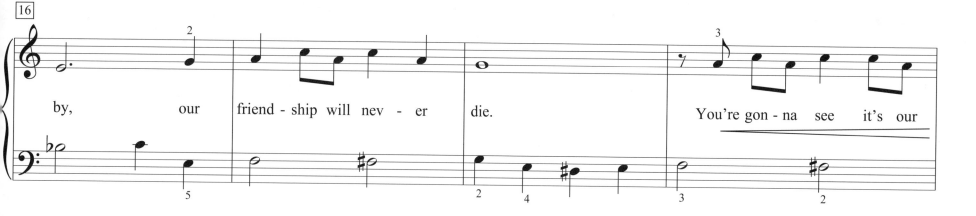

by, our friend - ship will nev - er die. You're gon - na see it's our

des - ti - ny. You've got a friend in me. Yes, you've got a friend in me.

EASIEST PIANO COURSE
Supplementary Songbooks

Fun repertoire books are available as an integral part of **John Thompson's Easiest Piano Course**. Graded to work alongside the course, these pieces are ideal for pupils reaching the end of Part 2. They are invaluable for securing basic technique as well as developing musicality and enjoyment.

John Thompson's Easiest Piano Course

00414014 Part 1 – Book only $6.99
00414018 Part 2 – Book only $6.99
00414019 Part 3 – Book only $7.99
00414112 Part 4 – Book only $7.99

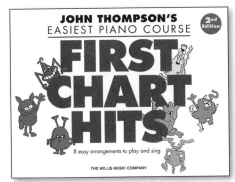

First Beethoven *arr. Hussey*

00171709 .... $7.99

First Chart Hits – 2nd Edition

00289560 .... $9.99

First Disney Songs *arr. Miller*

00416880 .... $9.99

Also available:

First Children's Songs *arr. Hussey*
00282895 .... $7.99

First Classics
00406347 .... $6.99

First Disney Favorites *arr. Hussey*
00319587 .... $9.99

First Mozart *arr. Hussey*
00171851 .... $7.99

First Nursery Rhymes
00406229 .... $6.99

First Worship Songs *arr. Austin*
00416892 .... $8.99

First Jazz Tunes *arr. Baumgartner*

00120872 .... $7.99

First Pop Songs *arr. Miller*

00416954 .... $8.99

First Showtunes *arr. Hussey*

00282907 .... $9.99

WILLIS MUSIC

EXCLUSIVELY DISTRIBUTED BY

HAL•LEONARD